HAUNTED
BATTLEFIELDS

GETTYSBURG

HISTORY AND LEGEND
BY
RUSSELL ROBERTS

PURPLE TOAD PUBLISHING

HAUNTED BATTLEFIELDS

ANTIETAM by Russell Roberts

GETTYSBURG by Russell Roberts

LITTLE BIGHORN by Earle Rice Jr.

VERDUN by Earle Rice Jr.

PUBLISHER'S NOTE
The data in this book has been researched in depth, and to the best of our knowledge is factual. Although every measure is taken to give an accurate account, Purple Toad Publishing makes no warranty of the accuracy of the information and is not liable for damages caused by inaccuracies.

ABOUT THE AUTHOR
Russell Roberts has researched, written, and published numerous books for both children and adults. Among his books for adults are *Down the Jersey Shore, Historical Photos of New Jersey,* and *10 Days to a Sharper Memory.* He has written over 50 nonfiction books for children. Roberts often speaks on the subjects of his books before various groups and organizations. He lives in New Jersey.

Printing 1 2 3 4 5 6 7 8 9

Publisher's Cataloging-in-Publication Data
Publisher's Cataloging-in-Publication data
Roberts, Russell.
  Gettysburg / Russell Roberts.
    p. cm.
Includes bibliographic references and index.
ISBN 9781624691126
1. Gettysburg, Battle of, Gettysburg, Pa., 1863—Juvenile literature. 2. United States—History—Civil War—1861-1865—Campaigns. 3. Gettysburg National Military Park (Pa.)—Juvenile literature. I. Series: Haunted battlefields.
 E475.53 2015
 973.7349
Library of Congress Control Number: 2014945188   ebook ISBN: 9781624691133

CONTENTS

CHAPTER

ONE

CURIOUS TIME

It was a warm night on the Gettysburg Battlefield—a summer's night filled with the sound of crickets chirping and owls hooting. Mice scurried through the tall grass and moths darted to and fro. The air was steamy and humid, hanging in place like a sheet on a clothesline. Up in the sky, the moon peered down like a giant eye, bathing the battle's monuments and statues with pale light.

It was a curious time for a single Civil War reenactor to be out. Virtually all reenactments are done during the bright light of day. It was even stranger for him to be seen without more of his comrades nearby.

Yet there he was, with nothing but the moonlight to guide him, slowly making his way on horseback down the rocky hill known as Little Round Top. He was dressed in the butternut-colored uniform of a Confederate officer.

As the figure got farther down the hill, the mist that often springs up and envelops the battlefield at night suddenly appeared, and the figure slowly began dissolving into it. Then, just before he vanished, it was plain to see that he had no head.

Like the mysterious rider that sometimes emerges, there's no telling what may suddenly appear on the Gettysburg battlefield—especially at night.

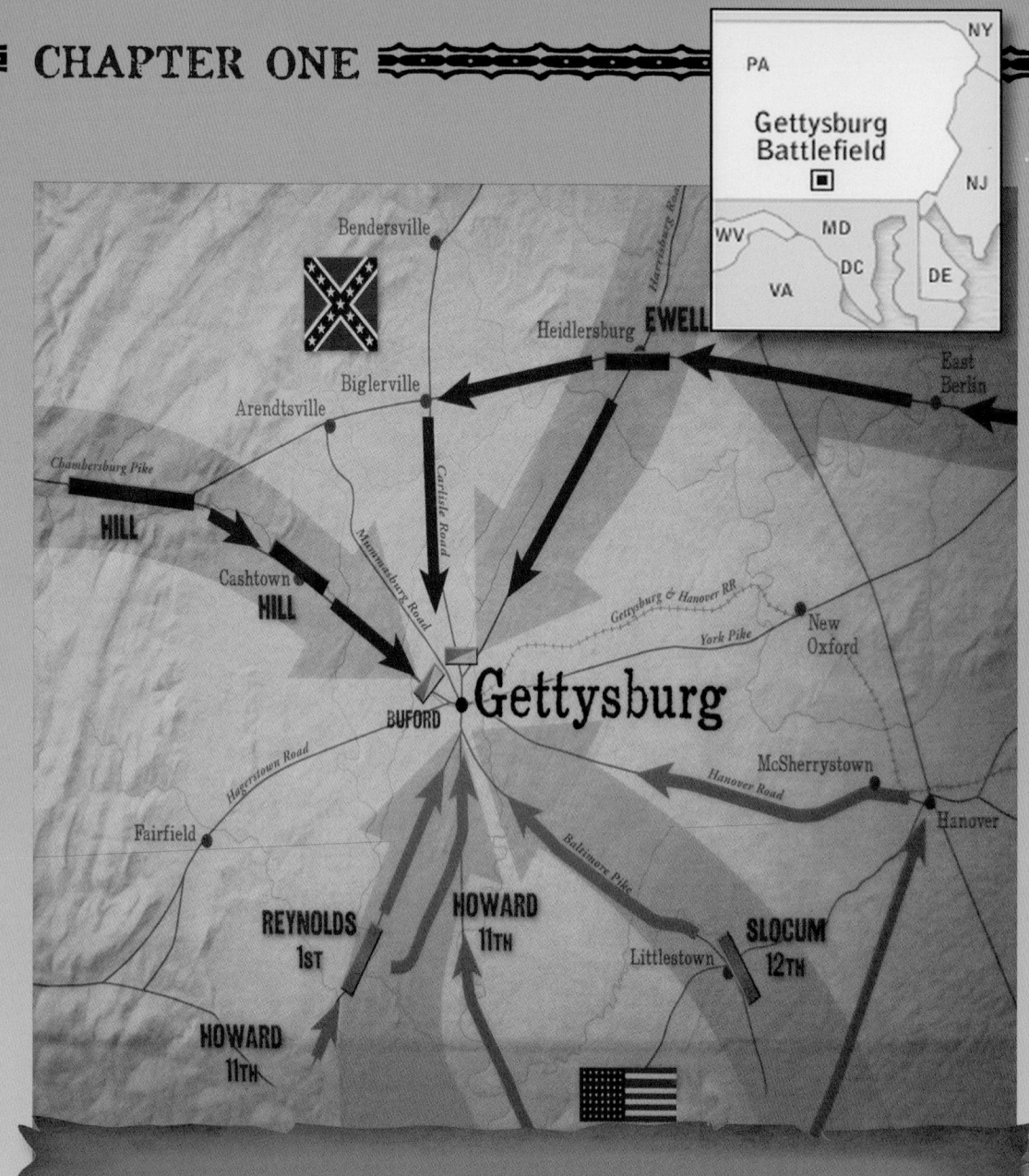

Gettysburg wasn't supposed to be a battleground. However, once the fighting broke out there, Union and Confederate forces from all over rushed to join in. Before long, both armies were completely involved.

The Battle of Gettysburg was the largest battle ever to take place in North America. It occurred from July 1 through 3, 1863, in the Pennsylvania town of Gettysburg. It happened during the American Civil War, also known as the War Between the States. More Americans—620,000—died in the Civil War than in all the other wars America has been involved in before and since.

By the summer of 1863, the Civil War had been raging for over two years. At first, many thought the war would be over quickly. However, it only got bloodier and bloodier. Confederate General Robert E. Lee proved to be a smart, tough fighter, who won numerous battles and defeated a parade of Union generals. Although their forces dwindled, the Union soldiers kept fighting, as President Abraham Lincoln searched for a general who could defeat Lee. Fortunately, the Union was successful in the western part of the country, where it won important victories.

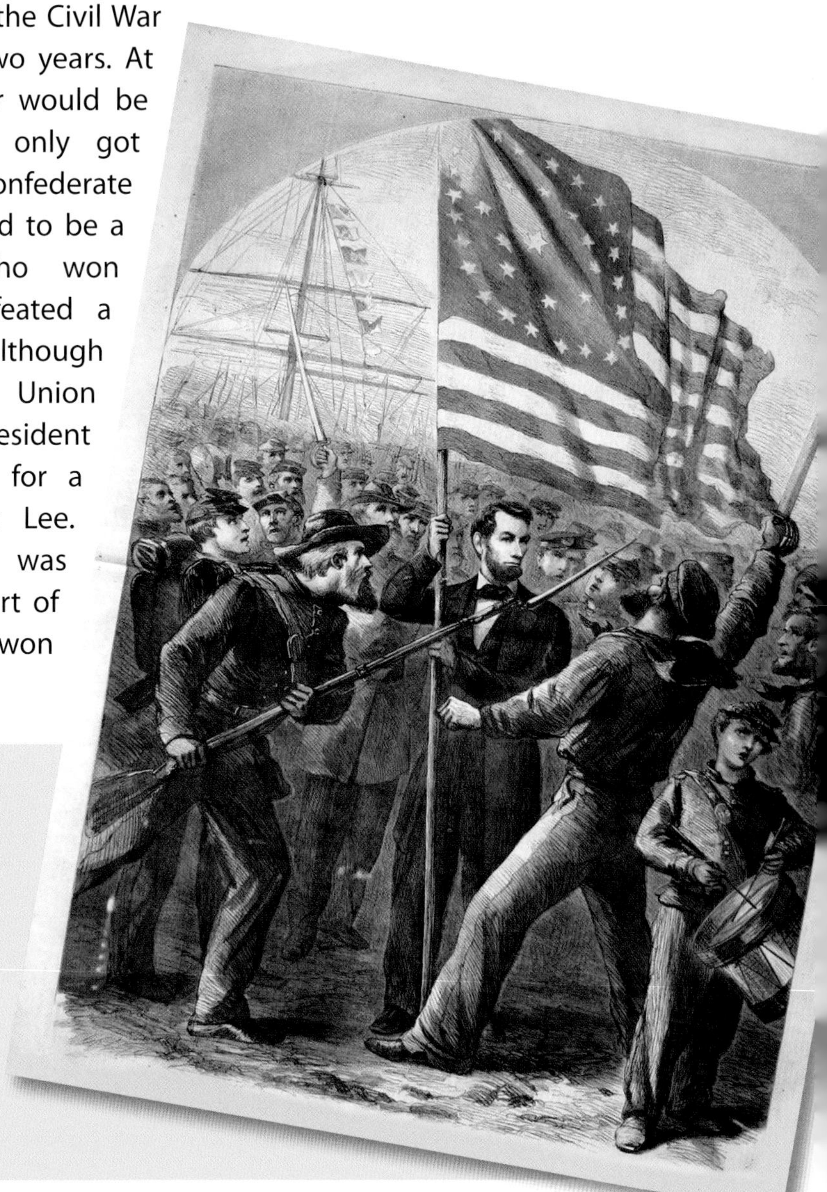

Stirring appeals to patriotism were necessary for both sides. As the war got bloodier and bloodier, casualties increased and more men were needed to fight.

By the time the fight came to Gettysburg, neither side had pulled ahead of the other. The Battle of Gettysburg would prove to be a turning point in a war that began in order to preserve the Union and later became a crusade against slavery.

The battle would also become the event that produced one of the most haunted places in America.

No one knows where ghosts come from or if they even exist. If they do, however, perhaps one reason is the sheer violence and suddenness of war. One minute a soldier is alive, the next he is dead, often in a violent, abrupt way. As the site of an epic battle, Gettysburg certainly saw its share of sudden, brutal deaths. Other battlefields throughout the world have also experienced unusual activity.

At the Sedgemont battlefield in England, flicking lights and the sound of voices have been reported. Soldiers are reported to suddenly rise up out of the mist and then sink back into it again. At Culloden in Scotland, there have been reports of two phantom armies in the sky, still fighting and dying as they did hundreds of years ago. In Croatia, numerous witnesses claim to have seen soldiers marching in the sky, led by an officer with a flaming sword. Ghosts of Roman soldiers from centuries ago have been sighted in the English town of York. In 1951, near the seacoast town of Dieppe in France, two women experienced a recreation of a battle on the Dieppe beaches that had occurred almost ten years before during World War II. For three hours, they listened to the screams of dying men, the thunder of artillery, and the shouted commands of soldiers that were nowhere in sight.

If these things have happened on other battlefields, perhaps it is not surprising that strange and unexplainable events have occurred in Gettysburg, where so many men died suddenly and horribly.

Although the official battlefield is that which is managed by the National Park Service, the three-day fight took place throughout the town. Men fought and died in just about every place in Gettysburg. Paranormal activity can be found virtually anywhere.

There are houses, too numerous to count, in which objects fall without explanation; strange glowing shapes are seen, and heavy footsteps, as if made by military boots, are heard where no people walk. There are phantom soldiers, whose marching feet can still be heard, yet when one looks out the window no

one is there. There are mysterious figures that appear for just moments, and then vanish when approached.

Even events that occurred after the battle seem to have become part of the eerie, psychic energy that pervades Gettysburg. Spangler's Spring is where, legend has it, men from both the Union and Confederate armies got water to refresh themselves during the battle. Now the spring is haunted by a woman in white—a spurned lover who committed suicide there in the 1880s. Numerous people have reported seeing a mysterious, glowing shape at the spring ever since the woman's death—a phantasm who is fated to return, again and again, to a place of restless energy.

Does a mysterious woman in white haunt this location of Spangler's Spring, where reportedly soldiers from both sides got water during the three hot days of fighting?

After the battle, the town of Gettysburg was littered with dead and dying men. The stench of death was so great that ladies were forced to cover their noses with their handkerchiefs.

At times, the entire town of Gettysburg is said to carry a strong smell of peppermint and vanilla. These are the same scents ladies supposedly dipped their handkerchiefs in, pressing them to their noses to cover the reeking stench of death as they walked about town after the battle.

This is Gettysburg—one of the most significant places in America, and also one of the most haunted.

Prior to the battle that would forever change a nation, Gettysburg was just another one of a thousand small towns in the United States.

The story of Gettysburg began in 1736. The family of William Penn (founder of Pennsylvania) bought land in southeastern Pennsylvania from the Iroquois Native American tribe. In 1761, Samuel Gettys opened a tavern near what would become Gettysburg. Twenty-five years later, Gettys's son, James, plotted a town there. It contained 120 lots and a central square around where the tavern existed. In 1800, the Pennsylvania legislature named a new county in the area as Adams County, after then president John Adams. Gettysburg became the county seat of Adams County.

Gettysburg had fertile farm fields, plenty of water, and rolling hills. It quickly attracted many settlers and farmers from the east. In 1860, Gettysburg contained 2,400 people. Ten roads led into Gettysburg from all directions, making it a transportation hub and helping to spur its growth. Among the businesses contained in Gettysburg were carriage manufacturing, shoemaking, and tanning.

This was the town that the Union and Confederate armies came upon in July 1863.

William Penn stands with open arms to greet Native Americans.

CHAPTER

TWO

A DATE WITH DESTINY

How did Gettysburg become the site of the biggest battle of the Civil War?

On May 15, 1863, Confederate President Jefferson Davis summoned General Robert E. Lee to a strategy conference in Richmond, Virginia. A bit earlier, Lee had stated that "We should assume the aggressive," and now he proceeded to demonstrate just how he intended to do that.[1] He would invade the North with his army, which was as large and powerful as it had ever been—about 75,000 men strong. The Army of Northern Virginia was coming off two stunning defeats of the federal army at which it had inflicted heavy losses: Fredericksburg (December, 1862, over 13,000 Union casualties) and Chancellorsville (May, 1863, 14,000 Union casualties). It seemed as if Lee's army could not be beaten, and that's what he believed.

There were many benefits to Lee's invasion plan:

1. It would change the scene of the fighting from war-ravaged Virginia.
2. It would enable Lee's troops to feed his army in Yankee territory, on Yankee food he seized.

★ ★ ★ ★ ★ ★ ★ ★ ★ ★ ★ ★ ★ ★ ★ ★

Confederate general Robert E. Lee was not afraid to take risks with his army against Union forces that were often superior in number. This had led the South to numerous victories against the North.

3. It would strengthen the so-called Peace Democrats, who were those in the North who wanted to bring an end to the fighting.
4. It would discredit Lincoln and the Republicans, who would be seen as stubbornly fighting a war they could not win.
5. Another victory over the Yankees might make England, France, or both, recognize the Confederacy, which might help it receive much-needed aid from those countries.
6. Finally, having a major Confederate army wreaking havoc in the North might very well force Lincoln to seek peace.

Davis gave his blessing to the idea, and so in early June, Lee marched his army north. Initially, it seemed as if all was going according to plan. The invasion caused panic in the North. Overseas, southern sympathizers in both England and France pushed for Confederate recognition. ". . . Everybody looks to Lee to conquer recognition," wrote a southerner in London, England.[2]

Jefferson Davis and his Confederate Cabinet. Left to right: Judah P. Benjamin, Stephen Mallory, Christopher Memminger, Alexander Stephens, LeRoy Pope Walker, Jefferson Davis, John H. Reagan and Robert Toombs.

When the Confederates invaded Pennsylvania it caused towns all over the state to worry that the rebels would wreak havoc in their community, such as what happened here in Chambersburg.

As far as finding food, the Confederate army had never eaten so well. As one southern general complained, if the rebel soldiers kept eating so much, "we will all get fat here."[3]

In late June 1863, the Army of Northern Virginia was moving through southeastern Pennsylvania. Lee did not initially pick Gettysburg as the place where he would fight a major battle against the Union Army. It became the site of this important battle by accident. As mentioned earlier, it was a town where ten major roads came together; it was almost impossible to avoid Gettysburg while traveling through southeastern Pennsylvania. However, the town carried no special military significance.

That was about to change.

The rebels had the best of it during the first day's fighting at Gettysburg, and with their recent run of successes against the federal army, they had to be feeling confident that they were on the verge of another victory.

Historians disagree on why Confederate troops entered Gettysburg on the morning of July 1. Some say it was to get a supply of shoes in the town. Others say the rebels were probing for information. Either way, when Confederates commanded by General Henry Heth approached the town, they were surprised to find Union cavalry troops under the command of General John Buford waiting for them. The two sides began shooting at each other. Then, like ants drawn to sugar, troops from both armies began rushing there to join in the fight.

First, however, some of them had to face the supernatural . . .

It was the night of July 1, 1863. The sun had gone down a few hours before, and darkness settled over the countryside. A thick screen of trees lined both sides of the road, cutting off any light from passing houses the soldiers could have used to see. Except for the feeble glow of some lanterns they carried, the men were completely blind. Mist arose, wrapping around the long column of soldiers that wound their way along like a giant slithering worm. The men talked and joked as they marched.

The soldiers were members of the Union Army's V Corps. They were traveling along a road that led to Gettysburg. As they marched along the dirt road in the darkness, some of the men in the front saw a figure in white mounted on a horse up ahead by the side of the road. He was urging the men forward, sweeping his arm ahead gesturing for them to hurry. He would ride forward, ahead of the column, and repeat the gesture.

Finally, the column caught up to the mysterious mounted figure. As the men looked at him, they stared in disbelief. Some passed their hand over their eyes, as if to clear them. Others rubbed their eyes and then stared again at the figure. It couldn't be. It couldn't possibly be. Yet it was.

The figure was that of George Washington, who had been dead for over 60 years.

Many Union soldiers reported seeing the figure of George Washington—dead for over a half-century – leading them forward.

Little Round Top was a stubby little hill that played a key role in the second day's fighting at Gettysburg.

There could be no mistake as to his identity. His features were familiar to everyone because of all the paintings and portraits made of Washington that were hanging in homes and businesses throughout the United States. He was dressed in the clothes of a past time: A tricorn (three-pointed) hat, long cape, and the uniform of a soldier from the American Revolution—a war that had ended decades before.

Word spread like wildfire from the front of the column to the rear. Some did not question that the ghost of George Washington was there. Instead, they took it as a good omen . . . a sign that Washington was watching over them.

The ghostly figure led the soldiers to the top of a hill named Little Round Top on the outskirts of Gettysburg. Then it vanished. The next day, July 2, Little Round Top and the V Corps's presence there would play a critical role in the fighting.

Did George Washington return from the grave to help the soldiers of the country he had fought so hard for? The story was considered so believable that Secretary of War Edwin Stanton conducted an investigation.

When asked about it, Joshua Lawrence Chamberlain, one of the Union soldiers who defended Little Round Top and a highly-educated man who would become governor of Maine, said:

"We know not what mystic power may be possessed by those who are now bivouacking with the dead. I only know the effect, but I dare not explain or deny the cause. Who shall say that Washington was not among the number of those who aided the country that he founded?"[4]

Robert E. Lee would have chosen another place to fight rather than Gettysburg if he had been given a choice. One very important reason he likely would have done so is because his cavalry was absent for much of the battle.

Before modern forms of communication, armies used cavalry to gather information. Cavalrymen rode in front of an army and scouted upcoming territory to see what lay ahead. If an enemy army was there, the cavalry could check it out, get an idea of its size and strength, and then report back.

The Confederate cavalry was under the command of James Ewell Brown (J.E.B.) Stuart. A dashing, flamboyant, and fearless soldier, Stuart was one of the reasons the Confederate army had been successful so far in the war. He had infused rebel horse soldiers with his leadership and charisma, and the southern cavalry became far superior to anything and anyone in the Union—out-riding and out-fighting everyone.

However, during the Gettysburg campaign, Stuart failed Lee. On June 9, Stuart was almost defeated by the Union cavalry at the Battle of Brandy Station. On June 25, perhaps to erase the embarrassment of his poor performance, Stuart took off on a ride around the Union Army to gather intelligence and supplies and to wreak havoc. What he actually did was deprive Lee of his cavalry and its ability to gather intelligence about the enemy at a critical moment. Without Stuart, Lee was "blind"—he had no way of knowing where the Union Army was, or its size and strength, or what the landscape was like in front of him.

If Stuart had been present, would Lee have picked Gettysburg as the place to fight?

James Ewell Brown Stuart

CHAPTER

THREE

"THE DEVIL TO PAY"

On the morning of July 1, 1863, Confederate troops approaching Gettysburg found Union cavalry troops under General John Buford waiting for them. Buford had seen Confederate soldiers just outside of town the day before. He knew that they'd be back the following day, and so he was there to meet them.

Although outnumbered, Buford's men had an advantage over the rebels. They had new, fast-firing weapons called carbines that fired so quickly it seemed like there were far more soldiers there than there actually were. Thus, they were able to hold off the Southerners for a while, and that allowed Union troops under Major General John F. Reynolds to arrive.

Dark-haired with a dark beard, Reynolds was considered one of the best generals in the Union Army. He rode up to Buford.

"What's the matter, John?" Reynolds asked Buford.[1]

"The devil's to pay!" replied Buford, meaning that this little fight was quickly growing bigger and more violent.[2] Just minutes later, as Reynolds was getting his troops in line for battle, he was shot

★ ★ ★ ★ ★ ★ ★ ★ ★ ★ ★ ★ ★ ★ ★ ★ ★ ★

Reynolds (left) and Buford were two Union commanders who played key roles in the first day's battle at Gettysburg.

Reynolds was killed by a Confederate sharpshooter early in the first day's fighting. According to some, his restless spirit still remains at Gettysburg.

dead by a Confederate sharpshooter. His body was quickly removed from the field.

But that doesn't mean Reynolds completely left Gettysburg. People who visit the Reynolds Death House (also known as the George George House) where the general's body was taken, report seeing strange floating orbs and figures of men in Civil War uniforms. Objects fall to the floor unexpectedly and things are not quite what they seem.

Both Confederate and Union troops poured into the area around Gettysburg. By early afternoon, about 24,000 Confederates faced about 19,000 Union soldiers. The northern troops were retreating through Gettysburg in confusion, and heading for the hills and high ground south of town. Arriving at the scene, Lee decided that this would be the place he would try to have his climactic battle with the Union forces.

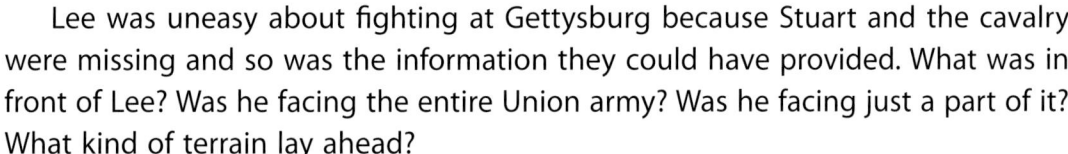

Lee was uneasy about fighting at Gettysburg because Stuart and the cavalry were missing and so was the information they could have provided. What was in front of Lee? Was he facing the entire Union army? Was he facing just a part of it? What kind of terrain lay ahead?

"I am in ignorance as to what we have in front of us here," Lee repeatedly said.[3] Though Lee did not like the situation, his men were there, and they seemed to be winning. So, he decided they would fight right there in Gettysburg.

There was one problem. The Union Army was occupying the hills and high ground south of town. The high ground was the best ground; the Union soldiers could easily see and shoot down at the Confederates. Therefore, Lee gave orders to one of his generals, Richard Ewell, to take those hills "if it were possible."[4]

But Ewell did not find it possible and did not order an attack. This led to one of the biggest what-if questions about Gettysburg (See sidebar). And so, the first day of fighting ended at Gettysburg with the Confederacy having lost a great chance for victory.

Apparently, though, not all the fighting had ended . . .

The failure of Confederate General Ewell to take some hills during the first day's fighting is considered a "what-if?" moment in the story of the Battle of Gettysburg.

Stone walls like this one provided welcome cover to soldiers trying to escape the hail of bullets during a battle such as Gettysburg.

A particularly brutal bit of fighting took place on a piece of high ground just outside of Gettysburg called Oak Ridge. Union troops occupied Oak Ridge, with the soldiers partially protected by a low stone wall. Thanks to an uncoordinated attack, hundreds of Confederate soldiers from North Carolina were cut down like blades of grass by northern soldiers. After the battle, the rebel soldiers' bodies were buried in long, shallow trenches. Exposed to the elements, the bodies quickly decomposed.

The area became known as Iverson's Pits, named after the North Carolina officer whose men were devastated in the battle. Years ago, the pits were part of a farm; and locals refused to go near them at night as the pits were shrouded in a mysterious mist.

Strange activity has also been recorded in the nearby woods. People report feeling anger, hatred, and overwhelming feelings of negativity there. Batteries in cameras and tape recorders often die out at the site, suddenly drained of all power—a typical sign of paranormal activity. And when the heat of the day is over and the evening mist rises up from the area like a shimmering white curtain, no one dares to get close. Strange activity has also been recorded in the woods near the pits where the stone wall was once located.

What lurks in the mist at Iverson's Pits and in the nearby woods? Is it the energy of men who remain present in this world after being so suddenly torn from it and hurled into the next?

The site of Iverson's Pits is considered one of the most haunted areas on the battlefield, and not a place for the faint of heart.

Does the spirit of a long-dead sentry sometimes appear in the cupola of this building?

Another haunting takes place in the cupola (a circular area on the top of a building) at the top of Pennsylvania Hall in Gettysburg College. Since it rests up high, this area was a popular lookout spot during the battle. (It is from here that Buford searched for Reynolds.)

Now, during some nights, a mysterious figure can be seen in the cupola looking out over the landscape as if still watching for past armies to appear. Known as "The Sentry," the figure marches back and forth in the cupola, still obeying orders given long ago by officers long dead. Even more frightening, sometimes the figure points its rifle at people on the ground as if it sees them.

Is this a case of a spirit from another time interacting with our world? Only the Sentry knows for certain, and nobody can get close enough to ask him.

History is not just a bunch of names and dates. One of the more fascinating aspects of history is the question, "What if . . . ?" What if Abraham Lincoln had stayed home the night he attended the theater and was assassinated? What if the South had won the Civil War? How would history have unfolded?

Another what-if question relates to the Battle of Gettysburg: What if Stonewall Jackson had been at Lee's side at Gettysburg? Would the battle have ended differently?

General Thomas Jonathan "Stonewall" Jackson was Lee's best general. He was extremely aggressive, and a fierce fighter. He was also a clever strategist, who excelled in the unexpected. Jackson was a big part of the reason why the Confederate Army had been so successful in the first two years of the war.

Two months before Gettysburg, Jackson had helped the South win perhaps its greatest victory over the North at the Battle of Chancellorsville. Unfortunately, he was accidentally shot by Confederate soldiers on the second day of the battle and died a week later on May 10, 1863, of pneumonia.

Some historians think that if Jackson had been with Lee at Gettysburg, he would have taken the hills that Ewell did not. If the hills had been taken, Lee might well have won the battle then and there. Lee himself said, "If I had Stonewall Jackson at Gettysburg, I would have won that fight; and a complete victory would have given us Washington and Baltimore, if not Philadelphia, and would have established the independence of the Confederacy."[5]

"Stonewall" Jackson

CHAPTER
FOUR
MISERABLE DEATH HOLES

The man looked unkempt—barefoot, with long stringy hair, and wearing ragged clothes with a big floppy hat—but two people visiting the Gettysburg battlefield during this sunny summer's day thought he was just a particularly effective reenactor. He stood atop one of the massive boulders that are strewn around a ten—acre section of the battlefield called Devil's Den.

Since the man looked so realistic, the people took some photos of him. As they were leaving the park, they asked a park ranger who that incredibly authentic-looking reenactor was.

The ranger looked at them strangely. He assured them there were no reenactors working there that day.

The people thought that odd, but dismissed it from their minds. When they returned home, they had their film developed, anxious to see how their pictures turned out.

But when they received their pictures, those taken of the reenactor were blurry and out of focus. Not one of the pictures of him had turned out clearly. The two people looked at each other, and a chill raced down both their backs. They knew that something

★ ★ ★ ★ ★ ★ ★ ★ ★ ★ ★ ★ ★ ★ ★ ★

Many visitors to Devil's Den on the Gettysburg Battlefield have reported seeing the spirit of a long-dead Confederate soldier among the jumble of boulders that make up the site.

paranormal had happened to them on that sunny day on the Gettysburg battlefield.

Those people were the latest to see "The Hippie," a spirit that prowls Devil's Den and has been seen by many people. He is often mistaken for a reenactor or a costumed guide with the National Park Service. The Hippie is dressed as many Texans were when they surged over Devil's Den during the white-hot battle on July 2, 1863.

Later, after the battle, the corpses of the dead lying all about Devil's Den were badly treated. They were reportedly dragged all about and placed in different poses so that photos could be taken of them. Perhaps the Hippie is one of those men, confused by the way he was treated in death and now comes to confuse others in life.

James Longstreet, Lee's most trusted general after Jackson's death, did not want the Confederacy to fight on July 2.

General James Longstreet's role in the Battle of Gettysburg has sparked controversy among historians for years.

General George Meade, the commander of the Union Army, arrived at Gettysburg on the evening of July 1 and decided to stay and fight it out with the Confederates.

All during the night, Union troops had been pouring into the Gettysburg area. They strengthened their positions on the high ground, and when daylight came, the Union troops were deployed in a three-mile long defensive line that resembled a fishhook. George Meade, commanding general of the Union Army, had also arrived on the scene.

Longstreet thought the Union's defense was too strong to attack. He urged Lee to pull the Confederate army around to the right and march toward Washington, D. C. That would force the Union to come out of its defensive positions and pursue them, and then the Confederates could choose the battlefield.

However, Lee rejected the idea. He was confident that his soldiers could defeat the Union then and there, as they had often done in the past. "The enemy is there, and I am going to attack him there," Lee said.[1]

Lee had wanted Longstreet to attack the Union as early in the day as possible. Perhaps because he did not believe in the attack, Longstreet did not get his men moving until four o'clock in the afternoon. What if Longstreet had attacked earlier? Would the Confederates have been successful?

When the Confederates finally attacked, the fighting was fierce in places with names that have since become famous, such as the Wheatfield, the Peach Orchard, Devil's Den, and Little Round Top.

On Little Round Top, troops under Joshua Lawrence Chamberlain repeatedly repelled Confederate attacks that, if they had been successful, would have put the rebels in control of the left side of the Union defensive position. It might have allowed them to destroy the entire Union army. After two hours of hard fighting, Chamberlain ordered a bayonet charge that routed the rebels and assured that Little Round Top would remain in Union hands.

In the Peach Orchard and Devil's Den, Confederates steadily pushed back Union troops under Daniel Sickles. Sickles had disobeyed Meade's orders and moved his troops out of the position he was ordered to take and into a new one.

The decision by General Daniel Sickles to disobey orders and move his troops to a new position on July 2, had disastrous effects for both him and his soldiers.

It was a weaker position, and the Confederates took advantage of it by battering Sickles's troops and forcing them back.

Sickles paid a high price for his mistake. He was wounded in the leg and it had to be amputated.

Some soldiers paid an even higher price . . .

Just north of the Peach Orchard was a hog farm run by Abraham Trostle. Dead and wounded men littered the ground around the farm.

A broken fence allowed some of the hogs to escape. Known to have a taste for human flesh, the hogs pounced on the humans lying on the ground. Those hurt, but still alive, tried to fight off these vicious animals with their bayonets. Wounded men, unable to move, were helpless victims of the ravenous beasts.

Today, the farm still stands on the battlefield. It is said that at night, the agonizing screams of the wounded men can be heard from the area around the farm, as the hogs attack and the men try desperately to fight them off.

Confederate attacks against the Union on Little Round Top and Cemetery Ridge gave the South its last opportunity on July 2. However, as the sun went down the two sides remained in the same places they had been when the day started. The Confederates had fought better, and Lee was certain that his men were about to break through the Union defenses, but the uncoordinated nature of the Confederate attacks had given the Union time to respond to each one.

As night fell and fighting ended, the makeshift field hospitals began working at a feverish pace trying to tend to the wounded. Amputation was the most common medical remedy during the Civil War (it accounted for 75 percent of all operations performed by Civil War doctors).[2] Rapid amputation was necessary in order to remove mangled limbs and stop infection from setting in, which would likely result in death if not treated. Called "miserable death holes" by one soldier, and compared to slaughterhouses, these field hospitals were marked by huge piles of amputated arms, legs, hands, and feet outside them.[3] The screams from wounded men in these hospitals became so loud the night of July 2 that bands were ordered to play loud music to drown them out.[4]

Perhaps it is not surprising that the locations of some of the field hospitals remain possessed by spirits of the dead. In these terrible places, where the

The peaceful appearance of the Weikert House hides the fact that many people believe it is haunted.

screams, cries, and agonies of wounded men rang out and their blood soaked the floors and splashed onto the walls, the life forces of men taken suddenly and violently from this world may still exist.

At the Weikert House, terrified Confederate soldiers hid in the attic, trapped there when the building became a Union field hospital. Now, the sound of boots nervously pacing across the floor above can be heard clearly from the bottom floor, even though no one is upstairs. People report feeling nervous, confused, and frightened there—all feelings that those Confederate soldiers must have felt knowing they were trapped in an enemy hospital. There is a door on the second floor that will not stay closed, even when nailed shut.

Wounded Confederate General William Barksdale was brought to the Hummelbaugh House where he begged for water as his life slowly ebbed away. His disembodied voice can still be heard, pleading for water. After Barksdale's death, his wife went to the house with the general's favorite hunting dog to claim his remains. When the dog reached Barksdale's grave, it fell to the ground, howling wildly. Now his disembodied voice can still be heard at the house, pleading for water. People know that the general's dog is keeping its eternal vigil at his grave.

This is Gettysburg, where the nightmare of war is over . . . but the memories never fade.

Imagine learning a few days before one of the biggest battles in history that you are in command of an army that will fight against that of Robert E. Lee, one of the greatest generals of all time. Now you have an idea of how George Meade felt!

Meade was placed in command of the Union Army on June 28, 1863, replacing Joseph Hooker. At forty-seven years old, Meade was a career soldier. He thought it unlikely he would ever take command of the Union Army because he had few political friends. Yet, President Lincoln, searching for a man who could challenge the formidable Lee, selected Meade after several other generals had turned him down (including John Reynolds, who was killed in the first few minutes of the Gettysburg battle).

Meade had little time to get comfortable in his new position. Lee had invaded Pennsylvania, and Meade had to pursue him. Arriving at Gettysburg on the evening of the first day, Meade conferred with his generals and decided that it was as good a place as any to fight Lee. During the next two days, Meade skillfully moved his troops around to defend against Lee's attacks.

Meade was later criticized for not pursuing Lee when the Confederate Army retreated after the battle ended. After the war, Meade became Commissioner of Fairmount Park in Philadelphia. He died in 1872.

George Meade thought he would never become commander of the Union Army, but when the opportunity came just before Gettysburg he proved a good choice.

CHAPTER

FIVE

PSYCHIC ENERGIES

On July 3, 1863, the third day of the Gettysburg battle, Lee was certain that the Union army was about to break. He had attacked the left and right sides of the Union's defenses, and knew that it had shifted troops to both sides to help fight off the Confederates. So, Lee reasoned that the center of the Union defenses were weak. If he attacked the center, Lee thought, his magnificent army could not fail to achieve the decisive victory he had been seeking since he entered Pennsylvania.

And so, Lee ordered Pickett's Charge—one of the most famous military actions in history.

Confederate General George Pickett, with 15,000 men, would attack the Union's center. However, General Longstreet had serious objections to the plan. The rebel soldiers would have to cross about one mile of open ground before they reached Union defenses. They would be subjected to Union artillery fire and then, when they got closer, to musket fire of the Union troops. In effect, the Confederate troops would be walking straight into a blazing fire with no place to take cover.

★ ★ ★ ★ ★ ★ ★ ★ ★ ★ ★ ★ ★ ★ ★ ★ ★

Are phantom armies still fighting one another at Gettysburg, engaged in a struggle that will go on until the end of time?

"It is my opinion that no fifteen thousand men ever arrayed for battle can take that position," Longstreet told Lee.[1]

But Lee did not want to hear objections. He thought Confederate artillery would disable many Union guns, and for two hours before the charge, 150 rebel artillery guns fired continually at Union troops. However, the Confederate aim was too high, and the Union forces suffered little damage.

Longstreet was still extremely reluctant to order the attack. When General Pickett asked if he should attack, Longstreet could not bring himself to tell him to do so. He merely nodded. "My feelings had so overcome me that I would not speak for fear of betraying my want of confidence to him," Longstreet later said.[2]

Around three o'clock p.m., about 15,000 Confederate troops stepped out of the woods and began advancing toward Union defenders a mile away.

Confederate General George Pickett's troops participated in the legendary and climactic Pickett's Charge, whose failure sealed the Confederacy's fate at Gettysburg.

Artillery was one of the factors that helped the North win at Gettysburg.

Unfortunately, what Longstreet had feared came to pass; the Union Army poured artillery and musket fire into the rebels so that they "literally mowed them down," as one Union soldier said.[3] Of all the Confederates who participated in Pickett's charge, scarcely half returned.[4] Lee looked forlornly at his decimated troops.

". . . all this has been my fault . . ." he said sadly.[5]

The Battle of Gettysburg was over. Between them, the Union and Confederate armies suffered about 50,000 casualties. The next day, July 4th, Lee and the Confederates began retreating.

Sadly, the battle ended too late for one woman. Twenty-year-old Jennie Wade was baking bread for Union soldiers in the home of her sister on July 3. The home was in a dangerous area between Union and Confederate forces known as "No Man's Land." As Wade baked, a single bullet passed through two doors and struck her in the back, killing her. She was the only civilian to die during the battle.

Now, people who visit her home report smelling fresh bread baking, as if Jennie is trying to finish her task. Strange shapes have been seen in the house,

Some think the spirit of Jennie Wade, the only civilian killed during the Battle of Gettysburg, may still be present in the house.

and there is speculation that they might be of her. Jennie had been anxiously awaiting the day when her sweetheart, Jack, who had fought in another battle, would return home.

Perhaps she's still waiting and hoping.

The battlefield is quiet now. It is filled with hundreds of markers and statues, each denoting a place where brave men fought and died over 150 years ago. In the daytime, the battlefield is full of visitors who walk and drive along it. At night, however, the battlefield is a mournful place, filled with half-light and shadows, where nothing is as it seems and anything is possible.

Sometimes at night, people swear, when the shadows are long and there is complete darkness on the sleeping battlefield, figures and shapes come to life. Wait! There! In the shadows! Is that a figure of a man, dressed in a blue uniform? And there! Near the monument! What is that strange, glowing orb?

Are those marching footsteps in the distance?

This is Gettysburg—one of the most significant places in America—and one of the most haunted.

After Gettysburg, there was more bloody fighting to come. The Civil War went on for almost two more years. However, never again would the Confederate Army be strong enough to invade the North. After Gettysburg, the Confederate States of America began a long, slow descent that ultimately resulted in its demise.

The incredible loss of life during the three-day battle at Gettysburg has had a lasting effect.

Although built in 1911, well after the battle, Stevens Hall, part of Gettysburg College campus, is a good example of how paranormal activity can be found all over Gettysburg.

The building was used for many years as a female dormitory. Supposedly, one cold winter's night, a young orphan boy was taken in by some female students on the third floor of Stevens Hall. The dorm's house mother unexpectedly knocked at the girls' door. Frantically, the girls searched for a hiding place in the room for their young friend. Finding none, they did the only thing they could think of and had him crawl out of the room's window. They told him to stay perched on its ledge, exposed to the bone-chilling cold and icy winds, until the danger passed.

The house mother stayed for a long time, talking to the girls. When she finally left, they raced to the window and threw it open, but the boy was nowhere to be found. He was never seen again.

After that, the girls and other students began seeing the face of a young boy floating outside their windows, looking in at them. However, when they opened them there was nothing there. The boy's face looks blue, as if he has been outside in the cold for hours. Not surprisingly, the students have named him "The Blue Boy."

In Gettysburg, the aftermath of the battle affects everyone and everything.

The "Blue Boy"

1801	Thomas Jefferson becomes the third president of the United States.
1803	The United States buys the Louisiana Territory from the French. It comes to be known as the Louisiana Purchase.
1804	Aaron Burr shoots Alexander Hamilton in a gentlemen's duel.
1807	Robert Fulton's steamship, *The Clermont,* makes its first voyage.
1812	The United States declares war on Great Britain.
1814	Francis Scott Key writes "The Star Spangled Banner."
1821	Emma Hart Willard opens the Troy Female Seminary, the first institution in the United States to offer higher education for women.
1831	William Lloyd Garrison publishes the first issue of *The Liberator,* the first publication dedicated to the emancipation of slaves.
1836	The Alamo falls.
1838	Fourteen thousand Cherokees are forced to march from western Georgia and southeastern Tennessee to Oklahoma. Four thousand die along the way. Their journey comes to be known as the Trail of Tears.
1846	The Mexican-American War begins.
1849	Elizabeth Blackwell becomes the first woman to receive a medical degree in the United States.
1852	Harriet Beecher Stowe publishes *Uncle Tom's Cabin,* which sells over a million copies in one year.
1860	Abraham Lincoln is elected president. In response, South Carolina secedes from the Union.
1861	The Civil War begins.
1863	President Lincoln signs the Emancipation Proclamation. Slaves in parts of Florida, Louisiana, and South Carolina are immediately freed.
1865	The Civil War ends. President Lincoln is assassinated.
1869	The Transcontinental Railroad is completed.
1876	George Armstrong Custer loses the Battle of the Little Bighorn, which comes to be known as "Custer's Last Stand."
1879	Thomas Edison invents the light bulb.
1886	The Statue of Liberty, a gift from France, is unveiled.
1891	James Naismith invents basketball.
1898	The Spanish-American War begins.

CHAPTER NOTES

Chapter Two

1. Stephen W. Sears, *Gettysburg*. (Boston: Houghton Mifflin Company, 2003), p. 7.

2. James M. McPherson, *Battle Cry of Freedom*. (New York: Oxford University Press, 1988), p. 651.

3. Stephen W. Sears, *Gettysburg*. (Boston: Houghton Mifflin Company, 2003) p. 108.

4. Haunted Places in Gettysburg, http://haunted-gettysburg.com

Chapter Three

1. Shelby Foote, *The Civil War: A Narrative: Fredericksburg to Meridian*. (New York: Vintage Books, 1986), p. 468.

2. Ibid.

3. Stephen W. Sears, *Gettysburg*. (Boston: Houghton Mifflin Company, 2003) p. 184.

4. Ibid, p. 229.

5. Kenneth C. Davis, *Don't Know Much About the Civil War*. (New York: Harper Perennial, 1996), p. 299.

Chapter Four

1. James M. McPherson, *Battle Cry of Freedom*. (New York: Oxford University Press, 1988), p. 656.

2. Kenneth C. Davis, *Don't Know Much About the Civil War*. (New York: Harper Perennial, 1996), p. 230.

3. Stephen W. Sears, *Gettysburg*. (Boston: Houghton Mifflin Company, 2003), p. 353.

4. Ibid.

Chapter Five

1. Stephen W. Sears, *Gettysburg*. (Boston: Houghton Mifflin Company, 2003) p. 357.

2. Earl J. Hess, *Pickett's Charge: The Last Attack at Gettysburg*. (Chapel Hill, NC: The University of North Carolina Press, 2001), p. 161.

3. Editors of Time-Life Books, *Voices of the Civil War: Gettysburg*. (Alexandria, VA: Time-Life Books, 1995), p. 120.

4. James M. McPherson, *Battle Cry of Freedom*. (New York: Oxford University Press, 1988), p. 662.

5. Earl J. Hess, *Pickett's Charge: The Last Attack at Gettysburg*. (Chapel Hill, NC: The University of North Carolina Press, 2001), p. 329.

 Further Reading

Books

Landau, Elaine. *The Battle of Gettysburg: Would You Lead the Fight?* Berkeley Heights, NJ: Enslow, 2009.

O'Connor, Jim. *What Was the Battle of Gettysburg?* New York: Grosset & Dunlap, 2013.

Olson, Kay M. *The Gettysburg Address in Translation: What It Really Means.* North Mankato, MN: Capstone Press, 2008.

Tarshis, Lauren. *I Survived #7: I Survived the Battle of Gettysburg, 1863.* New York: Scholastic Press, 2013.

Vansant, Wayne. *Gettysburg: The Graphic History of America's Most Famous Battle and the Turning Point of the Civil War.* Grand Rapids, MI: Zenith Press, 2013.

Works Consulted

Cavendish, Richard. *The World of Ghosts and the Supernatural.* New York: Facts on File, 1994.

Davis, Kenneth C. *Don't Know Much About the Civil War.* New York: Harper Perennial, 1996.

The bullet hole through Jennie Wade's door

Further Reading

North Carolina Monument in Gettysburg

Editors of Time-Life Books. *Ghosts: The Enchanted World*. Alexandria, VA: Time-Life Books, 1984.

Editors of Time-Life Books. *Hauntings: Mysteries of the Unknown*. Alexandria, VA: Time-Life Books, 1989.

Editors of Time-Life Books. *Voices of the Civil War: Gettysburg*. Alexandria, VA: Time-Life Books, 1995.

Foote, Shelby. *The Civil War: A Narrative: Fredericksburg to Meridian*. New York: Vintage Books, 1986.

Hess, Earl J. *Pickett's Charge: The Last Attack at Gettysburg*. Chapel Hill, NC: The University of North Carolina Press, 2001.

McPherson, James M. *Battle Cry of Freedom*. New York: Oxford University Press, 1988.

Nesbitt, Mark, and Patty A. Wilson. *Haunted Pennsylvania*. Mechanicsburg, PA: Stackpole Books, 2006.

Sears, Stephen W. *Gettysburg*. Boston: Houghton Mifflin Company, 2003.

Further Reading

On the Internet

150th Gettysburg

    http://www.gettysburgcivilwar150.com/

American Civil War: Invading the North

    http://www.historyofwar.org/articles/wars_american_civil_war05_invading_north.html

America's Most Haunted Places: Gettysburg Battlefield

    http://www.prairieghosts.com/gettysburg.html

The Gettysburg Address

    http://www.abrahamlincolnonline.org/lincoln/speeches/gettysburg.htm

Gettysburg: National Military Park

    http://www.nps.gov/gett/index.htm

Ghost Encounters at Gettysburg

    http://paranormal.about.com/od/hauntedplaces/a/gettysburg-ghosts.htm

Haunted Gettysburg and Her Ghosts

    http://www.essortment.com/haunted-gettysburg-her-ghosts-42457.html

Haunted Places in Gettysburg

    http://haunted-gettysburg.com/

bivouac (BIV-wok)—A military encampment of tents or other items.

casualty (KAZ-yoo-uhl-tee)—A member of the armed forces lost to death, wounds, sickness, capture, or unknown whereabouts.

charisma (kuh-RIZ-muh)—A personal power or quality that gives an individual influence or authority over others.

demise (dih-MYZE)—Death.

eerie (EAR-ee)—Strange and frightening.

envelop (en-VEL-uhp)—Surround entirely.

flamboyant (flam-BOY-uhnt)—Bold and showy.

formidable (FOR-mih-duh-buhl)—Forceful; powerful.

havoc (HAV-uhk)—Confusion; disorder.

infuse (in-FYOOZ)—To fill.

paranormal (payr-uh-NOR-muhl)—Not explainable by science.

pervade (purr-VAYD)—Spread throughout all parts of.

phantasm (FAN-taz-uhm)—A ghost.

psychic (SY-kik)—Outside of natural or scientific knowledge.

reenactor (ree-en-AK-tur)—Someone who recreates a historical character, such as a soldier in a battle.

rout—To defeat and cause a retreat.

thrash—To totally defeat.

vigil (VIH-juhl)—A period of watchful attention.